BOATS

BOATS

by Sunny Reynolds

COURAGE
BOOKS

AN IMPRINT OF RUNNING PRESS
PHILADELPHIA ▪ LONDON

9   8   7   6   5   4   3   2   1
Digit on the right indicates the number of this printing

Library of Congress Cataloging-in-Publication Number 2001094408

ISBN 0-7624-1264-X

Cover and interior design by Kathy Klingaman
Quotes researched by Jody Brady
Edited by Sara Phillips
Typography: Berkeley and Venetian

This book may be ordered by mail from the publisher.
But try your bookstore first!

Published by Courage Books, an imprint of
Running Press Book Publishers
125 South Twenty-second Street
Philadelphia, Pennsylvania 19103-4399

Visit us on the web!
www.runningpress.com

Cover image: Southern coast of Portugal
Overleaf: Bora Bora, French Polynesia
Opposite: Venice, Italy

D e d i c a t i o n

In memory of my parents, Lillian and Louis Porter.
They endured with grace and good humor.
And my sister, Cindy, who loved the sea and travel
and who was always patient while I waited
for that perfect light.

Help thy brother's boat across, and lo!
Thine own has reached the shore.

—Hindu proverb

Foreword

Despite its name, Earth is extraordinary because of water. Covering some 90 percent of the surface of the planet and penetrating on average two and a half miles into the oceans, water is the single element without which no life can exist. Life's deepest roots are aquatic, not terrestrial, and it is provoking to reflect on whether this life-giving vitality is at the core of man's proclivity to be in, on, or near water.

We are, as an intellectual, spiritual, adventure-seeking species, inextricably linked to water. From baptismal fonts to puddles, tropical reefs to bountiful seas, placid lakes to turbulent streams, crashing surfs to crushing depths, water is symbolic, sustaining, mysterious, mesmerizing, powerful, terrifying, fun.

We have exhibited endless ingenuity in designing vessels that take us on and into water. In vessels ranging from blunt-ended punts to graceful sloops, hydroplanes to submarines, pirate ships to oil tankers, we have invaded the watery realm, transporting, harvesting, exploring, and conquering. We go to the water seeking thrills, isolation, serenity, and relaxation.

My first "boat" was a rubber raft that my twin sister and I at age eight once paddled a half-mile off the South Carolina coast to join dolphins trailing a shrimp trawler. Next was the single-mast sailboat on which Cousin Rick would carry us offshore and then intentionally flip. Cast into the water, I imagined dangers looming large; on the raft or back on the sailboat I found utter security.

Above: Puerto Varas, Chile

There were to be many more boats in my life: I played in canoes and ski boats; I did volunteer work on commercial shrimp boats; and I studied marine fishes from the decks of small inflatable zodiacs, Boston whalers, and major ocean-going research vessels.

I have also journeyed to the depth of 3000 feet in the four-man *Johnson Sea Link II* research submersible during the filming of the Smithsonian's IMAX 3-D film, *Galapagos*. Nothing I've done rivals the thrill of descending in the sub to visit places and observe ocean creatures no other human has seen, trusting technology with my life.

The quiet yet physically dynamic photographs appearing in Sunny Reynolds' *Boats* capture the multitude of feelings, relationships and bonds that humans have with boats. The photos are in turn peaceful, confrontational, emotional and strong. The images from ports she has visited around the world are expressive portraits of Kenyan dhows, Peruvian reed boats, Venetian gondolas, Moroccan fishing boats, and vessels representing almost all sizes and traditions.

Sunny has combined skill with her camera, love of boats, and world travel into visual poetry. In turn, readers are encouraged to reflect on these scenes and let their own complexity of feelings about boats emerge.

Carole C. Baldwin, Ph.D.
Marine Biologist
National Museum of Natural History
The Smithsonian Institution

Northern Coast of Portugal

Sail forth into the sea,
O ship!
Through wind and wave,
right onward steer!

—from "The Building of a Ship"
by Henry Wadsworth Longfellow (1807–1882)
American poet

Left: Off the coast of Nantucket, Massachusetts
Overleaf: Boston Common, Boston, Massachusetts

*T*his sort of sea life is charged with an indestructible charm. There is no weariness, no fatigue, no worry, no responsibility no work, no depression of spirits. There is nothing like this serenity, this comfort, this peace, this deep contentment to be found anywhere on land. If I had my way I would sail on forever and never go to live on the solid ground again.

—from *Following the Equator*
by Mark Twain (1835–1910)
American writer

Above: Chiloe Island, Chile
Left: The Mediterranean Sea, off the coast of Turkey

*E*verything is made from the totora reeds themselves. The cut stalks are kept staked in the water to keep them flexible. The twine that binds them is stripped from the outside of the reed. The skill in building the boat is to know the thickness required to make the bundles of reeds waterproof and when and where to tie the twine that gives them their shape. All this is done by hand and eye. And even foot.

—from *Full Circle*
by Michael Palin (b. 1943)
English comedian and writer

Lake Titicaca, Peru

*T*he sea pronounces something, over and over, in a hoarse whisper; I cannot quite make it out.

—from *Teaching a Stone to Talk*
by Annie Dillard (b. 1945)
American writer and poet

Above: Montego Bay, Jamaica
Left: Quepos , Costa Rica

*O*nce more upon the waters! yet once more!

And the waves bound beneath me as a steed

That knows his rider.

—from "Childe Harold's Pilgrimage"
by George Gordon, Lord Byron (1788–1824)
English poet

Above: Inner Harbor, Baltimore, Maryland
Left: Valdivia , Chile

W ith a blacksmith do not wed;

so much washing will there be!

Marry a seaman, a sailor, instead;

he comes home laundered from the sea!

—Spanish rhyme

Above: Lamu, Kenya
Left: Vallarica, Chile

Above: Lamu, Kenya
Left: Off the east coast of Bali, Indonesia

Top and right: Essaouira, Morocco
Above: Asilah, Morocco

On the hundred yards of beach between houses and low surf, the people place coconut shells in little sand-pockets to hold arrangements of palm leaves, blossoms and rice. This keeps the sea spirits happy, but it also expresses the Balinese delight in bright colors and patterns. Besides the nets, the hulls of the catamarans, which serve as skiffs, are painted purple, orange, or blue, embellished with such specifics as a friendly animal eye.

—from *Their Father's Work: Casting Nets with the World's Fishermen* by William McCloskey (b. 1928) American writer

Northern coast of Bali, Indonesia

M y soul is of longing

for the secret of the Sea,

And the heart of the great ocean

Sends a thrilling pulse through me.

—from "The Secret of the Sea"
by Henry Wadsworth Longfellow (1807–1882)
American poet

Above: Playa Hermosa, Costa Rica
Right: Quepos, Costa Rica

*I*t isn't that life ashore
is distasteful to me.
But life at sea
is better.

—Sir Frances Drake (1540–1596)
English admiral and explorer

Coast of Southern California

*D*idst ever see a gondola? For fear

You should not, I'll describe it you exactly:

'Tis a long covered boat that's common here,

Carved at the prow, built lightly, but compactly,

Rowed by two rowers, each called 'Gondolier',

It glides along the water…

—from "Beppo"
by Lord Byron (1788–1824)
English poet

Right: Venice, Italy
Overleaf: Costa Brava, Spain

*T*he voice of the sea speaks to the soul. The touch of the sea is sensuous, enfolding the body in its soft, close embrace.

—from *The Awakening*
by Kate Chopin (1851–1904)
American author

Above and right: Lamu, Kenya

*I*need an ocean to teach me:

whatever it is that I learn—music or consciousness,

The single wave in the sea, the abyss of my being,

The guttural rasp of my voice, or the blazing

   resumption of fishes and navies—

so much is certain; even in sleep, as if

by the trick of a magnet, I spin on the circle

of wave upon wave of the sea, the sea's university.

—from "The Sea"
by Pablo Neruda (1904–1973)
Chilean poet

Bay of Islands, New Zealand

I'm on the sea! I'm on the sea!

I am where I would ever be,

With the blue above and the blue below,

And silence wheresoe'er I go.

—from "The Sea"
by Bryan Waller Procter (1787–1874)
English poet

Above: Off the coast of southern California
Right: City park in Paris, France
Overleaf: Barcelona, Spain

The first morning I went I woke at predawn and it was like the beginning of the world, silent water, silent sky. The little dawn wind swept across the deck and the Pleiades were misty at the horizon.... At night we moored in coves, where there was nothing but our own boat, so small it seemed lost under the great black space.... There was silence there and had been since men first plied these waters.

—from *Turkish Reflections*
by Mary Lee Settle (b. 1918)
American writer

The Black Sea, off the coast of Turkey

*T*here is nothing—absolutely nothing—half so much worth doing as simply messing about in boats. In or out of 'em, it doesn't matter. Nothing seems really to matter, that's the charm of it. Whether you get away, or whether you don't; whether you arrive at your destination or whether you reach somewhere else, or whether you never get anywhere at all, you're always busy, and you never do anything in particular; and when you've done it there's always something else to do.

—from *The Wind in the Willows*
by Kenneth Grahame (1859–1932)
English author

The Mediterranean Sea, off the coast of Turkey

I cross'd on the boats, often up in the pilot-houses where I could get a full sweep, absorbing shows, accompaniments, surroundings. What oceanic currents, eddies, underneath—the great tides of humanity also, with ever-shifting movements. Indeed, I have always had a passion for ferries; to me they afford inimitable, streaming, never-failing, living poems.

—from "My Passion for Ferries"
by Walt Whitman (1819–1892)
American poet

Victoria Harbor, Mahé Island, Seychelles

*A*s soon as we anchored in Matavai Bay, we were surrounded by canoes.... Within the reef there is an expanse of smooth water, like that of a lake, where the canoes of the native can ply with safety and where ships anchor.

—from *Voyage of the Beagle*
by Charles Darwin (1809–1882)
English naturalist and writer

Left: Bora Bora, French Polynesia
Overleaf: Valparaiso, Chile

W hen the wind shifts against the sun,

Trust it not for back it will run.

When the wind follows the sun,

Fine weather will never be done.

With rain before the wind

Stays and topsails you must mind,

But with the wind before the rain

Your topsails you may set again.

—English sailing lore

Above: Inner Harbor, Baltimore, Maryland
Right: Chesapeake Bay, Virginia
Overleaf: Vancouver, British Columbia

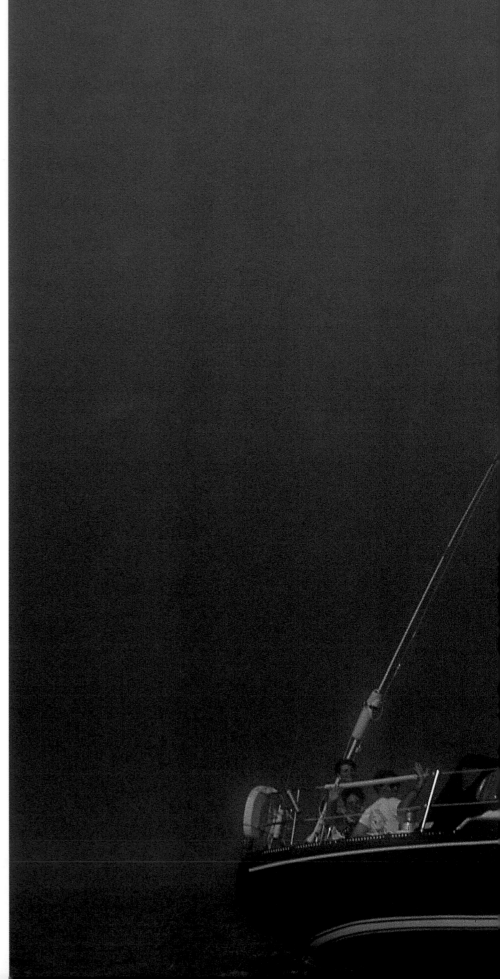

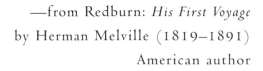es! Yes! give me this glorious ocean life, this salt-sea life, this briny, foamy-life, when the sea neighs and snorts, and you breathe the very breath that the great whales respire! Let me roll around the globe, let me rock upon the sea, let me race and pant out my life with an eternal breeze astern and endless sea before!

—from Redburn: *His First Voyage*
by Herman Melville (1819–1891)
American author

Top: Baltimore Harbor, Maryland
Bottom: San Francisco, California
Right: Chesapeake Bay, Virginia

One day as I went along the shore, I saw that all the boats were beached, and the slack water period of the early afternoon prevailed. Nothing was going on, not even the most leisurely of occupations, like baiting trawls or mending nets, or repairing lobster pots; the very boats seemed to be taking an afternoon nap in the sun.

— from *The Country of the Pointed Firs*
by Sarah Orne Jewett (1849–1909)
American author

Puerto Varas, Chile

*H*ow lovely the boats look as they turn to face the gentle breezes in a sunny harbour, or motor smoothly in and out of port. The fishermen in their woollen caps and sea rig are so rugged, so picturesque.

—from *The Portuguese: the Land and its People*
by Marion Kaplan (b. 1946)
English photojournalist and writer

Southern coast of Portugal

*N*othing could be more absolutely certain than that we are enjoying ourselves. One can not do otherwise who speeds over these sparkling waters and breathes the soft atmosphere of this sunny land. Care cannot assail us here. We are out of its jurisdiction.

—from *The Innocents Abroad*
by Mark Twain (1835–1910)
American writer

Right: Quepos, Costa Rica
Overleaf: Nantucket, Massachusetts

*I*n spite of love

this dream:

to go alone

to where

the fishing boats are empty

on the beach

and no one knows

which man is

father, husband, victim,

king, the master of one cage.

—from "Family Pictures"
by Mervyn Morris (b. 1937)
Jamaican poet

Above: Bar Harbor, Maine
Right: Eastern coast of Jamaica

Above and right: Lake Titicaca, Peru

F rom time to time the launch passed through choppy waters where the warmer Mediterranean current disagreed with the waves moving in from the Atlantic. Small whitecaps broke and hissed in the dark alongside, and the boat, heaving upward, would remain poised an instant, shuddering as its propeller left the water, and then plunging ahead like a happy dolphin.

—from *Let It Come Down*
by Paul Bowles (1910–1999)
American writer and composer

Above and left: Essaouira, Morocco

Seine River, Paris

With the fishermen and the life on the river, the beautiful barges with their own life on board, the tugs with their smoke-stacks that folded back to pass under the bridges…I could never be lonely along the river.

—from *A Moveable Feast*
by Ernest Hemingway (1899–1961)
American novelist

*T*he steamer, like a huge shuttle, wove in and out among the countless small islands; its long trailing scarf of grey smoke hung heavily along the uncertain shores, casting a shadow over the pearly waters of the Pacific, which swung lazily from rock to rock in indescribable beauty.

—from *Legends of Vancouver*
by E. Pauline Johnson (1862–1913)
Canadian poet

Above: Vancouver Harbor, British Columbia
Right: Chesapeake Bay, Virginia

*T*he sea being smooth
How many shallow bauble
boats dare sail
Upon her patient breast

—fom *Troilus and Cressida*
by William Shakespeare (1564–1616)
English dramatist and poet

Off the coast of Villarrica, Chile

*A*pparently the builder of a boat acts under a compulsion greater than himself. Ribs are strong by definition and feeling. Keels are sound, planking truly chosen and set. A man builds the best of himself into a boat—builds many of the unconscious memories of his ancestors.

—from *The Log from the Sea of Cortez* by John Steinbeck (1902–1968) American author

Above and left: Essaouira, Morocco

Off the coast of Lamu, Kenya

*A*dhow was on its way from Lamu to Zanzibar, following the coast about a mile out....The air was like that of a hothouse, and so damp that all the planks and ropes of the boat were sweating a salt dew. The heavy waters sang and murmured along the bow and stern.

—from *Seven Gothic Tales*
by Isak Dinesen (1885–1962)
Danish author

*I*beg my dear will not be uneasy at my staying out so long. To
be sure I lose the fruits of the earth, but then I am gathering the
flowers of the sea.

—from a letter to his wife
Edward Boscawen (1711–1761)
English admiral

Above and left: Lake Titicaca, Peru

*O*God, thy sea is
so great,
And my boat is
so small.

—Breton fisherman's prayer

Above: Southern Lake District, Chile
Right: Essaouira, Morocco

I will not close my eyes, neither those in my head nor those in my soul, as the ship carries me away, along with my future, my dreams, and my beliefs....Like our distant ancestors in the age of migration we are on a voyage of discovery, a journey toward a new land and life.

—from *The Mute's Soliloquy: A Memoir*
by Pramoedya Ananta Toer (b. 1925)
Indonesian author

Jakarta, Java, Indonesia

When a man goes to sea, he ought to give up thinking about things on shore. Land don't want him no more. I've had me share of things go wrong and all come from the land. Now I'm through with the land and the land's through with me.

—from *The Long Voyage Home*
by Dudley Nichols (1895–1960)
American screenwriter

Columbia River, Washington
Overleaf: Milford Sound, New Zealand

Left: Costa Brava, Spain
Above: Northern coast of Bali, Indonesia

*S*ome carpenters were at work here mending a scow on the green and sloping bank. The strokes of their mallets echoed from shore to shore, and up and down the river, and their tools gleamed in the sun a quarter of a mile from us, and we realized that boat-building was as ancient and honorable an art as agriculture, and that there might be a naval as well as a pastoral life.

—"A Week on the Concord and Merrimack Rivers"
by Henry David Thoreau (1817–1862)
American writer and naturalist

Valparaiso, Chile

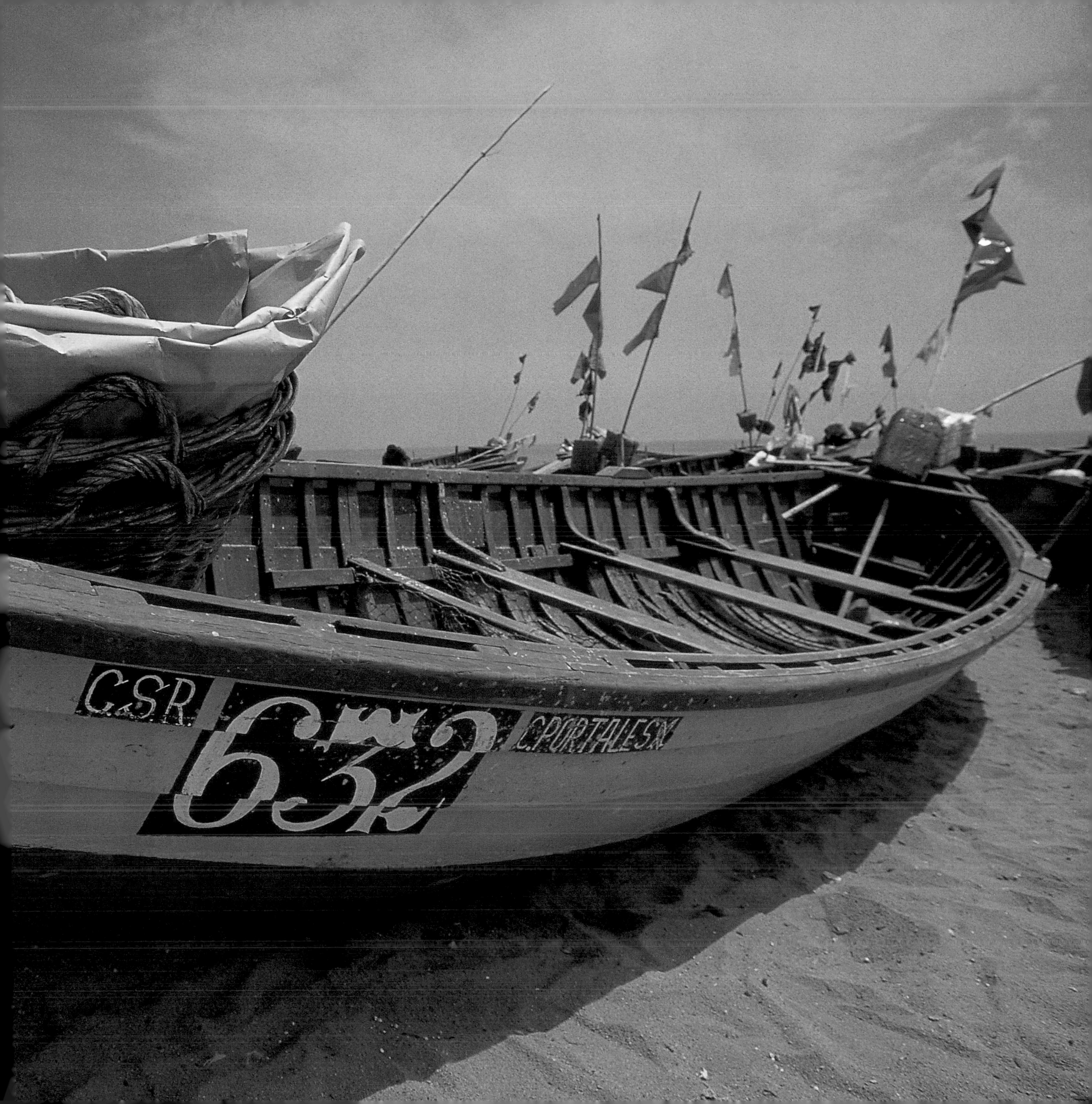

C.S.R
632
C.PORTALES N.

*T*he boat, at the speed of a darting fish, sprayed drops of salty water over his face, rosy with happiness and sunshine… The ocean was a copy of the sky in a slightly darker tone, and the crests of foam were like brushstrokes breaking the monotony of the color.

—from "The Blue Fish"
by Julieta Pinto González (b. 1922)
Costa Rican author

Pacific coast of Costa Rica

*U*nder a broken sky the bay had a soft metallic sheen, blown into a million coins by the wind. A hundred fishing boats lay on the water like dabs of paint.

—from *God and Mr. Gomez*
Jack Clifford Smith (1916–1996)
American author

Above: Southern coast of Turkey
Right: Essouira, Morocco

On an early morning such as this, all the world still pale, the stars fading in the sky, evanescent wisps of vapor rising slowly from the unruffled surface of the water, the sea seems to come into its own, displaying more than ever its vast unbounded might.

—from *The Sea-Crossed Fisherman*
by Yasar Kemal (b. 1922)
Turkish author

Right: Baltimore, Maryland
Below: Baja California, Mexico

*S*ome of the corners where our way branched off, were so acute and narrow, that it seemed impossible for the long slender boat to turn them; but the rowers, with a low melodious cry of warning, sent it skimming on, without a pause.

—from *Pictures From Italy*
by Charles Dickens (1812–1870)
British Author

Above: Venice, Italy
Left: Murano, Italy

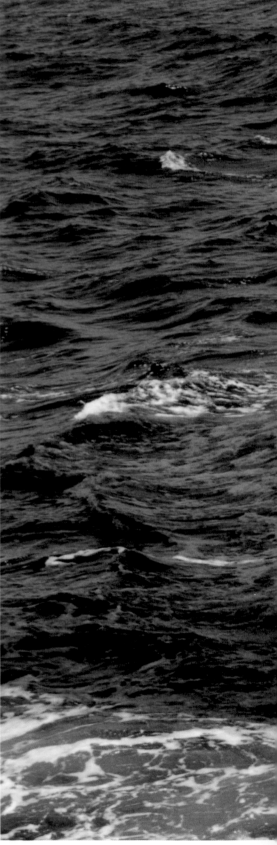

*T*he sea! The sea! The open sea!

The blue, the fresh, the ever free!

—from "The Sea"
by Barry Cornwall (1787–1874)
English poet

Above and left: The America³ competing in the America's Cup, San Diego, California

Above: Bay of Islands, New Zealand
Right: Barcelona, Spain

The sea is large. The sea must know more than any of us.

—from "The Sea Hold"
by Carl Sandburg (1878–1967)
American poet

Top: Praslin Island, Seychelles
Above: La Digue Island, Seychelles
Right: Off the northern coast of Bali, Indonesia

*T*o cross the sea is to submit to the sea

Once venture out and you belong to it

All you know is the sea

All you are the sea

—from "Shoriken"
by Charles Brasch (1909–1973)
New Zealand poet

Milford Sound, New Zealand

Above: Bali, Indonesia
Right: Jakarta, Java, Indonesia

*V*essels large may
venture more,
But little boats should
keep near shore.

—from *Poor Richard's Almanac*
Benjamin Franklin (1706–1790)
American statesman and writer

Above: Cleveland, New York
Left: Off the coast of Quepos, Costa Rica

*T*he inhabitants have numerous canoes built and fitted with much skill and neatness. In these they pay their visits from island to island, and at the close of a party it sounds rather novel to a stranger to hear "Madame Chose's canoe!" instead of carriage announced as in waiting.

—from *Narrative of Voyages*
by Captain William Fitzwilliam Owen (1774–1857)
Canadian ship's captain

La Digue Island, Seychelles

*S*o we beat on, boats against
the current, borne back
ceaselessly into the past.

—from *The Great Gatsby*
by F. Scott Fitzgerald (1896–1940)
American author

Above: Java, Indonesia
Left: Southern coast of Peru

Above: Ralun, Chile
Right: Basque region of Spain
Overleaf: Montego Bay, Jamaica